Let's Fly a Kite

Richard Tan

Rosen Real Readers

Rosen Classroom™
New York

This is my kite.

My friends and I like to fly kites.

It is windy outside.

It is a good day to fly a kite.

My friends and I go
to a large field.
There are no trees around.
This is a good place
to fly a kite.

We are ready to fly our kites.
I hold the spool of string
with my right hand.
I hold the line with my left hand.

I let go of the line.

The line gets longer.

It unwinds from the spool.

I hold the spool tight.

I run with my kite!

My friends run, too.
We run through the field.

Our kites get caught
in the wind.
They rise to the sky.

The lines unwind from our spools.

The lines get longer.

Our kites go higher!

Look at our kites in the sky!

It is fun to fly a kite!

Words to Know

field

kite

string

windy